Edition Schott

Lee Hoiby

b. 1926

Last Letter Home

for Baritone and Piano
für Bariton und Klavier

ED 30017
ISMN M-60001-048-6

www.schott-music.com

Mainz · London · Madrid · New York · Paris · Prague · Tokyo · Toronto
© 2008 SCHOTT MUSIC CORPORATION · Printed in USA

Preface

Jessie Givens, Private First Class, US Army, drowned in the Euphrates River on May 1, 2003, in the service of his country, in his 34th year. He wrote a letter to his wife, Melissa; five year-old son, Dakota, nicknamed "Toad"; and his unborn child, Carson, nicknamed "Bean." He asked Melissa not to open the envelope unless he was killed. "Please, only read it if I don't come home," he wrote. "Please, put it away, and hopefully you will never read it."

to the fallen in Iraq
Last Letter Home

Text: Jesse Givens

Lee Hoiby, Op. 71

© 2008 Schott Music Corporation, New York

4

You are my an - gel, soul - mate, wife,____ lov -

- er and best friend.____ I am so sor - ry.____ I

did not want to have to write this let - ter. There is so much more I

need to say, so much more I need to share. A

Af - ter you tuck the chil - dren in, give them hugs and kiss - es from me.

Go out - side and look at the stars,_____

go out - side and look at the stars, and count them.

Don't____ for - get to smile._____

6 April, 2006
dur.: 6' 30"